FILL THE DAM THING UP!

Building Connections:
Communicating Throughout the Lifecycle of Infrastructure Projects

Mary Ellen Miller, APR

*Note: this is a phrase used by the owners of Boomtown & Co., a store in Johnson City, Tennessee. Owners sold merchandise with that phrase throughout the project. "Fill the dam thing up" became a battle cry of sorts with project engineers and geologists gleefully wearing ball caps with that slogan into meetings and prominently displaying T-shirts and caps in their offices. The project was completed both on time and under budget.

Fill the Dam Thing Up!
Building Connections:
Communicating Throughout the Lifecycle of Infrastructure Projects

By Mary Ellen "Mel" Miller, MarketingMel
MarketingMel Publications

Copyright 2023

TVA Disclaimer: "Any views and opinions that I may express in this manuscript/book are attributable to me personally and do not represent the opinions of my employer (Johnson Service Group) or the company for which my employer was providing services (Tennessee Valley Authority)."

Table of Contents:

Prologue vii

Introduction - Your Communications Playbook ix

CHAPTER 1
History: An Aging Infrastructure Problem 1

CHAPTER 2
A Muddy Seep: The Clock is Ticking 5

CHAPTER 3
Project Leaders: Be Confident 11

CHAPTER 4
Tools of the Trade: Welcome Others 15

CHAPTER 5
Be Strategic 19

CHAPTER 6
Stakeholders: Partners and Social Media 23

CHAPTER 7
The Media 27

CHAPTER 8
Everyone is an "Expert" 31

CHAPTER 9
A Diverse, International Project, Chewing Tobacco, and "The American Way"......... 33

CHAPTER 10:
Prepare for the Unexpected: From Break-ins to Blow-ups...................................... 37

CHAPTER 11
Safety Rules: Pink Hardhats and Dressing for Success 41

CHAPTER 12
Pro Tips: Scan Environment, Keep it Clean! 43

CHAPTER 13
Social Media and Public Outreach... 47

CHAPTER 14
Kindness and Ethics 49

CHAPTER 15
Benchmarking and Focus Groups 51

CHAPTER 16
The Very Rich: Your Neighbors and "the Golden Rule" 53

CHAPTER 17
Transferrable Skills for Any Infrastructure Project 55

CHAPTER 18
Tearing Down, Starting Over 59

CHAPTER 19
Tracking Progress: Spreadsheets and Plan B 63

CHAPTER 20
The Power of Dreams 67

Epilogue: Have a Vision 71

SPECIAL COVID INSERT
COVID-19: Working Through a Global Pandemic 75

Author's Note 83
Acknowledgements 85
About the Author 87

Prologue

June 30, 2022

It was a classic late June day in Northeast Tennessee. It was only 9:30 in the morning, but the sun was already beating down overhead. I arrived early and found a metal picnic table located in some shade at the dam's recreational area. I perched on top of the table and looked out at the water, including the beach and swimming area. The earthen embankment stood as a backdrop. I was early for a 10:30 media interview, which gave me plenty of time to observe this place that had been my work home for nearly seven years.

Out of the corner of my eye, I noticed a large, lone RV tucked into the far corner of the parking lot. Soon, I looked up and heard children's laughter coming from that direction. I turned my head in time to see a family, dressed in swim attire, making their way down the grassy hill toward the lake. The children were giggling as they carried swim noodles in their arms. One young boy wore an inner tube around his waist as he skipped down the hill toward the sand and water. Soon, they were splashing in the lake's swimming area that bordered the sandy beach. Before long, other swimmers arrived and joined in the fun. A floating orange rope and a line of red and white buoys kept the swim area separated from passing boaters. Two swimmers did laps along the rope, occasionally hanging on the lane line to rest. I watched the scene of frolicking in a lake on a hot summer day and smiled, recalling the long hours of hard work it took to get here.

▶ **viii** Fill the Dam Thing Up!

INTRODUCTION

Your Communications Playbook

As I reflect on my career in public relations, I realize it's actually been a series of projects: build-ups and teardowns. Whether it's a major infrastructure project or a local political campaign, the public relations professional finds him/herself in the middle of a swirling hub of activities. The counselor will listen to, and become the confidante of, the project manager and senior leaders and sit in the meetings as highly technical language is bantered about. He or she will soak in the language of the project and translate it into words the common man can understand.

And then it ends and everyone moves on to the next client or the next project.

With the help of the tips outlined in this publication, you will have the communications playbook!

▶ x

CHAPTER 1

History: An Aging Infrastructure Problem

The last huge reservoir, New Melones, was built in California on the Stanislaus River in Calaveras County. The Army Corps of Engineers cut the ribbon on it in 1979.

The Problem: Our Nation's Aging Infrastructure and My "Why"

The United States is full of aging infrastructure.

It is also full of angry neighbors, residents, and "influentials" who are always quick to shout "NIMBY!" ("not-in-my-backyard"), no matter the project.

And our country is full of communications professionals. PR pros like you, for whom this book is written, who are looking for sound advice from a communications pro who has been in the trenches. Here is the story of communicating one major U.S. infrastructure project. I hope the knowledge I acquired there can benefit other communicators working across the country and the world.

▶ 2 Fill the Dam Thing Up!

"Built to Last" vs. "Father Time"

Out of all the earthen dams in the world, 6-7 fail per year. Half of them are in international locations. Typically, in the United States, dams are "built to last" about 50 years. However, the dam builders came from "the greatest generation." As they toiled with their slide rules to make the calculations necessary to construct some of America's finest and well-known dams, they built something that, in most cases, lasted much longer.

The dam where I worked as lead communicator was built in the early 1950s to help harness a river in order to prevent devastating flooding and generate hydropower.

It lasted 63 years. Then a sinkhole and a "muddy seep" were discovered at the base of the dam. While all dams leak, in this case, a direct correlation was discovered between the "muddy seep" (defined as muddy water carrying soil particles) at the base of the dam and the elevation of the reservoir above the dam. When the reservoir was rapidly lowered approximately ten feet, the "muddy seep" disappeared. The pressure of the water against the earthen dam was removed. All points indicated the dam was showing signs of internal erosion, one of the top two causes of dam failure in the world. (The other issue is "overtopping," defined as water "exceeding the crest of a dam.")

With either scenario, a dam failure can have serious and potentially deadly consequences. Keeping a dam and the people downstream safe are of paramount importance. Dam safety is even observed in the United States each May 31 on National Dam Safety Awareness Day. The date commemorates the failure of the South Fork Dam in Johnstown, Pennsylvania in 1889. According to the Federal Emergency Management Agency, the Johnstown disaster was the worst dam failure in the history of the United States, with over 2,200 lives lost.

Bridge Collapse in Pittsburgh

As I was writing this book on communicating infrastructure projects, a terrible real-life example occurred. A bridge in Pittsburgh, collapsed just prior to President Joe Biden's visit to town to discuss America's aging infrastructure and the bipartisan infrastructure bill. Such irony. A human chain was formed to help survivors, who were perilously dangling from a Port Authority bus off the side of the bridge. Ten people were injured and three were hospitalized. Thankfully, no one was killed in this harrowing example of infrastructure failure.

The bipartisan infrastructure bill was passed and, as I write, we await the budgeting process. For the people crossing bridges in Pittsburgh, that time cannot come soon enough!

Dam Conversations with Old Friends

We had a group of friends who got together and had dinner regularly during my college years at Cornell. Some of them had been dorm-mates freshman year. I was a transfer student, but they kindly welcomed me to their group. Several of the guys were engineering students. Forty years later, during the coronavirus pandemic, one member of the dinner gang decided we should hold a virtual reunion. We were eager to sign on and the first call had a good turnout. There was the usual catching up on life after four decades, then we all agreed to have another call.

The second call found the somewhat stilted earlier conversations falling away, and it was like we were back at college, swapping ideas across the dining table at Noyes Hall.

"So, I am planning to write a book about infrastructure communications," I said over Zoom, waving my pocket-sized copy of *Start Writing Your Book Today* by Morgan Gist MacDonald in front of my laptop's camera.

"When is the last time a dam was built in this country?" responded an old friend, rather rhetorically. He had spent his career as an engineer-turned-marketer for a Fortune 500 company.

"Ah," I said. "You're right. We have an aging infrastructure problem."

SUMMARY:

- Aging infrastructure is a national crisis.
- Pay attention to the world around you through environmental scans. What's happening in infrastructure near you?
- Listen to old college buddies when you get an opportunity and if you're still in college, cultivate friends in other majors. One day, years later, you may appreciate their wisdom and insights.

CHAPTER 2

A Muddy Seep: The Clock is Ticking

This is the story of how I shaped the communications for one of the largest infrastructure projects in America from 2015- 2022. Best of all, it was located just a 25-minute drive from my home!

The Story Begins: The Issue

In October 2014, a sinkhole was discovered in the parking lot of the dam's control building. A short time later, a dam safety inspector noticed a muddy seep at the base of the earthen embankment. Those two issues together meant possible internal erosion; again, it's the number two cause of dam failure in the world. Dye testing indicated there was a direct pathway from the reservoir above, to the river below. There was no time to waste in securing the dam and ensuring the safety of the people downstream. The reservoir above the dam was lowered approximately ten feet below its normal winter pool level. Once the water was lowered, the pressure on the embankment was removed and the seepage stopped.

Working in Real-Time: The Clock is Ticking!

When the internal erosion issue was discovered at the dam, the immediate reaction was to kick into crisis communications mode. Dam failure was not an option. Once the reservoir above the dam was lowered to take the pressure off the earthen embankment above the dam, the work began in earnest. The analogy that we as communicators used was "building a house." If you were building a new house, you would probably hire an architect or builder, draw up plans, purchase the land and maybe even clear it before unveiling your new home drawings to your friends. Heck, you might even pour the foundation!

In this case however, solutions were created in real time. On a project of this magnitude, the clock is ticking. There was even a countdown clock (think NASA here) in the main conference room. Every day, project leaders looked at a red digital reminder of their ultimate time goal: to get the project completed safely within the five-to- seven-year timeframe, an expectation that was shared with the public. The bar was set, now the challenge lay ahead: managing expectations!

Construction and engineering teams, with consultation from the world's leading dam safety experts, put their heads together and went to work creating the plan. After looking at several options, one design was selected. To put it in simple terms, the ultimate "fix" was a composite seepage barrier. An underground wall was built with overlapping 50-inch-diameter concrete pilings drilled up to 170 feet underground. That portion of the project would be its highly visible centerpiece. The wall - along with a grouting and drilling program and rock buttress fortifications - would "cut off" the internal erosion within the earthen embankment.

Cross-Functional, Internal Communications Teams

Shortly after the leak was discovered at the base of the dam, the communications team moved into full crisis communications mode. I was not a contractor on the project yet, but the team's supervisor created a cross-functional internal team led by the project manager. The team met monthly to stay abreast of the latest developments at the dam.

The project was of particular interest to the stakeholder representatives. Working with government officials and customers, the message was then carried to the general public through key influencers in the community. The natural resources team was also a key player in the cross functionality, as they were the original owners of the site and it would eventually return to them. For seven years, the public would not have access to the beach area they loved at the dam. Instead, a temporary beach was created as an interim measure. The final year the water came up, inundating the temporary beach, while the project transitioned to its end.

Angry Neighbors and the Challenge of PR

When I joined the project team, residents were already furious. I attended the Lake Association meetings where the president sat with his arms folded, scowling at me. He barely acknowledged my presence as the lead communicator for the dam project. People understandably get angry when you take down the level of their beloved lake.

During normal times, in order to prevent flooding, a team of engineers gradually moves the lake up and down about ten feet, depending on the season. After Labor Day, additional water is released downstream and the pool is held at "winter" levels to accommodate snow and rainfall. Lake residents expect that cycling. When the water level was brought down seven to ten additional feet below normal winter pool levels, people were angry.

If I told members of the general public what I did for a living they would exclaim, "Who would want to do that?"

That was the question I received when I first heard about the opening for a community relations program manager for one of the largest infrastructure projects in the world.

"Why would anyone want to do *that*?" asked my dentist as my mouth was propped open.

"You're doing *that*?" asked other friends who worked in professions that I would consider far more stressful.

"Yes!" I exclaimed and I loved it.

Boats on Lifts vs. Human Life Downstream

The project was ultimately about safety. A major plant was located on the river downstream – as was a city. We could not afford the risk of a dam failure for the safety of the people living and working below the dam.

"What about our boats?" cried many of the residents upstream. Since the incident happened in the fall with the lake descending to winter pool, many residents were preparing to remove boats from their lifts to winterize them. However, the reservoir had to be lowered rapidly to take pressure off the earthen embankment. The estimated time of repair was not yet known. Some boats were left hanging in the air simply because people did not realize the gravity of the situation and the time involved in the repair. Although I was not yet working on the project, it's my understanding that there was no time for lengthy reminders about boats, with the safety of people downstream possibly in jeopardy. I clearly remember one of our silver-haired, eloquent leaders saying there was no comparison between saving a boat and saving a life. Quick, dramatic precautions were necessary to ensure safety downstream. While we all had empathy for the residents whose boats were stranded, the potential loss of life and property downstream was a risk we could not take.

As we learned, the free market moves in. We began to hear of companies that would - for a price - remove the stranded boats from their lifts.

SUMMARY:

- The clock is ticking on a major infrastructure project. You will work in real-time, often with all aspects of the project visible.
- Create a cross-functional, internal team led by the project manager and meet regularly to provide updates. Have your project manager lead the call.
- Be prepared for inquisitive comments — even when in the dentist's chair!
- No matter the project, safety should always come first.

▶ 10 Fill the Dam Thing Up!

CHAPTER 3

Project Leaders: Be Confident

Tips for Project Leaders:

"In preparing for battle I have always found that plans are useless, but planning is indispensable."
~ General Dwight D. Eisenhower

- Write a Plan, Work Your Plan, then Adapt!

In terms of communications, I started with an outline of a plan.

From there, I expanded it and prepared and updated the plan each year. In the short term, I used the "R-PIE" process I learned in my accreditation studies: Research, Plan, Implementation, Evaluation. That simple process, along with the "10-Step PR Plan" by Ferne Bonomi (https://www.online2learn.net/docs/APRPREP/Mod5/Readings/APR-Mod5-10-Step-Process.pdf), served as guideposts on the infrastructure PR Journey.

- Be Confident

One question I heard most often was posed to our project manager by the media and others: "Are you confident this proposed fix is going to work?"

The answer was always a resounding "Absolutely!"

The project manager must express utter confidence in the fix laid out before the public, as he/she is the lead spokesperson or "subject matter expert" (SME) for the project. In some ways, the SME is like an NFL quarterback. A calm, quiet attitude serves him or her well in the long run. Our project manager was also known to bring takeout to his hotel room rather than endure the barrage of questions from local restaurant patrons!

- **More on Confidence: "The Chameleon Effect"**

I once heard leadership guru Darren Hardy speak about the "Chameleon Effect." It is a nonconscious mimicry in which we adopt the behaviors and mannerisms of those around us. So, when the project manager is asked over and over, particularly by the media, how confident he is in the project, he exudes and radiates confidence. He states, "I am very confident." That, in turn, gives the media and the public the belief that the project is proceeding well.

- **Projects Come in Moveable, Interchangeable Parts**

Just like a Lego set or Jenga puzzle, a large infrastructure project has many components. "A" can come before "B," or sometimes "C" gets inserted before "B." The project management lingo for that is "critical path methodology," and it simply means noting which tasks must be checked off the list to complete the project on time. There is generally some flexibility with sequencing and scheduling of certain tasks. I had to learn how to communicate that. It did not mean the project was off its timeline; it just meant that whatever resources were available at the time came to the forefront ahead of another component part. This was key to project communications to prevent the public from becoming frustrated if they noticed one part of the project sequence move ahead of another.

- **Changing Players**

My father, who was a professional fundraiser and PR man, used to say, "The only thing constant is change." When it comes to the leadership of a major infrastructure project, those words ring true! I recall starting the project and taking a photo of the three (then) project leaders. As I write this and the project is ending, not one of them is still onsite managing the project.

In this case, they did such exceptional work that they were promoted and moved on to other projects. Likewise, the cast of co-workers on a project changes as the project evolves.

> **SUMMARY:**
>
> - Write a plan and work it! My personal favorite is the "Ten Step PR Plan" by Ferne Bonomi.
> - Be confident! Be sure your project leaders are confident, particularly before they go on camera.
> - Chameleon Effect - people will pick up on the confidence of the leader.
> - Some of the planned sequences made initially, may switch around. No worries, it's just a way to keep the project moving along.
> - Leadership will change on a project. It's inevitable.

▶ **14** Fill the Dam Thing Up!

CHAPTER 4

Tools of the Trade: Welcome Others

Have a Public Welcome Space

My office was in a trailer, as were all the project offices. Doublewides are temporary structures and even though the project ran for multiple years, the players and the companies they represented rotated in and out. In the case of the community relations trailer where I worked with two armed guards (there had been serious threats prior to my arrival), the public was welcome to stop by and learn about the project. I remember the local anchorman joking with me when he came out to do a story, "Mel, who would have ever thought you would say 'Come out to visit me in my trailer?'"

Create Visuals and Post Them

Easy-to-understand "cartoon" type graphics were created for the project. The problem was internal erosion; the fix was a composite seepage barrier with an underground cutoff wall as its main component. Additional phases of berm construction and a grouting program provided what the project manager often described as "belt and suspenders." These graphics were posted to the communications trailer walls. If one visual portion of the project ended up coming ahead of another, it was still easy to show the progress. The visuals were placed on the project website. We also provided the public with giveaway maps of the lake. We displayed the project's community relations awards, including a photograph of the magnificent bald eagle, whose "EagleCam" the agency supported financially. (A bald eagle couple nested on private property near the lake.)

Build a Model

The project could be a challenge to explain in words. One of my early communications "dreams" became reality with the creation of a 3D-model tabletop dam. A specialized team constructed the dam using LIDAR data and 3D printing. The tabletop dam was built like a puzzle. The earthen embankment portion of the dam was the puzzle piece, exposing the underground cutoff wall when removed. The model dam was so well-worn that the internal "cutoff wall" actually fell out of the dam right before a large event with students! Two local university professors came to my rescue. The team that created the dam, in another city, sent me a PDF of "the wall," the professors printed and cut it on their specialized equipment, and voila! We were back in business just before "showtime."

Children of all ages loved the model dam. Its high-level view of the lake above, and river below, gave them an immediate understanding of the project. One other model that helped immensely was the concrete cutoff wall itself. It was a miniature (if heavy!) version of the overlapping concrete piles. The model showcased the two "primary" piles, on the left and right along with one center "secondary" pile, of a different color. This overlapping concrete is what formed the "cutoff" wall construction that quite literally "cut off" the seepage. We took both models with us to school events and civic clubs throughout the region, using them as teaching tools.

SUMMARY:

- Welcome the public to a community space where they can learn about the project.
- Use visuals to tell the project story.
- If possible, build a model of the project – it works well for school groups and the public alike.

▶ 18 Fill the Dam Thing Up!

CHAPTER 5

Be Strategic

The Public Relations Pro as Trusted Counselor

Make a point to gain the trust and confidence of the project leads. One simple way to do this is to keep their confidences. Do not be a gossip. <u>Keep lips zipped!</u>

Once they saw my work and I gained their trust, the project team requested I take a "seat at the table." Participating in weekly management meetings is key to the communicator's understanding of the project. I used to say their weekly strategy sessions were the one time I saw the "sausage being made." The main team would never speak that openly in front of the contract construction crew. Sitting with the team and listening in, the communicator is privy to the inner sanctum. This enables the communicator to forecast potential communications hurdles the technicians might not otherwise see.

Join Public Relations Society of America (PRSA)

In my case, being a member of my professional organization helped me find the job.

My boss decided to "fish where the fish are," so to speak. It makes a lot of sense (particularly on a lake job where fishing is all-important). One month after a highly controversial and well-publicized public meeting, she put out a notice to our local chapter of the Public Relations Society of America (PRSA) that she was looking for a local PR person who was well-versed in the region, could speak on camera, and knew the community. And presto: there I was!

Like all good PR pros, I am an adrenaline junkie. So, during our local chapter's Public Relations Society of America meeting in August 2015, I heard that project leadership was looking for a person with local experience to lead community relations. I jumped at the opportunity. I had invited two college students with me that day. I recall telling the students on the drive home, "This project is a great opportunity!" It sounded like a PR person's dream: community outreach in times of crisis.

Being students, they were open to the possibility that I had not completely lost my mind to take on such a task, (as opposed to the reactions of so many of the professionals I knew).

Win Awards

I have always been an advocate for entering awards competitions. Sure, it's a hassle at the time to gather up entries, but once you win the award, it's there for life. YOU and YOUR TEAM are now award winners! As a project, we entered international competitions and won several major awards. As a member of the PRSA, I entered our work in the local chapter's awards program each year. You don't realize how much work is done throughout a year until you reflect at entry time. We won top awards each year for the community relations work we produced: video podcasts, e-newsletters, social media, videos, etc.

Be Inclusive

It was tough to be on a project far away from "the mothership." I remember the first 90 days being so rough that I thought if I could just get through that time, departing would not look too bad on my resume! I recall heading to the corporate office for occasional visits and "all hands" meetings. The first time I visited as a co-worker and colleague, when lunchtime rolled around, a steady stream of my new co-workers made their way across the small downtown park to a restaurant nearby. They did not extend an invitation to me. I tagged along anyway and began chatting with a colleague at the back of the line. He was also visiting from another location and in much the same "uninvited" predicament. We talked about looking for healthy eating alternatives and our mutual fondness for apples. We are fast friends to this day. *Tip to anyone in a position to greet new people to any organization: be sure to make them feel welcome and included!*

A Typical Day in the Life of a PR Pro on a Project: Prepare for Lonely Times

At times, the loneliness on the site was overwhelming. Unlike the project team that stayed far away from the public at a remote location on the site, I was officed in a public trailer at an intersection of two country roads. The public could access me and I could easily move in and out to public events, meetings, etc. I would get walk-in traffic, particularly on sunny Friday afternoons and more often during the early years of the project when it was still new. There was great interest in learning about the project (and heck, everyone likes to go for a drive along the lake on a sunny Friday afternoon!) I always welcomed people and showed them the project model and illustrations of the project that lined the trailer walls.

As I mentioned earlier, there were two armed guards with me. At the start of the project, someone had threatened to blow up the dam and that settled the need for full-time guards for the next seven years of the project. On sunny days, I ate my packed lunch at the picnic table outside my office. Then I walked circles in the small public parking lot for exercise, creating a labyrinth. As I walked and prayed, I waved to passing trucks towing boats and heading to the nearby boat ramp.

My only day-to-day interaction with the team was during our morning meetings or when I was called up top for a special meeting. I loved it when people would come to the site and visit me. Those were rare occasions and I remember the people well…professional fundraisers from charities the project was supporting or the occasional college student or businessman interested in learning more about this great infrastructure fix. I always appreciated them taking the time to meet me in my country trailer. I especially loved the break in solitude.

SUMMARY:

- Be a trusted counselor. Zip lips to gain leaders' confidence and a seat at the table.
- Join the Public Relations Society of America - my professional organization has helped me so much. Membership in it is how I found this job.
- Enter competitions and win awards for the work you do on the project.
- Be inclusive. When someone new shows up at any organization, welcome him/her.
- Be prepared. The work can sometimes be lonely, particularly if it's in a remote location.

CHAPTER 6

Stakeholders: Partners and Social Media

Stakeholders

Stakeholders are members of the community who have a vested interest in the project, including government officials - such as public office holders - and customers. They are the influencers who will take your messages out to the community and, in turn, share with you what they hear from community members.

We held separate updates for stakeholders just prior to our media updates, generally twice per year. We did not mix stakeholders and media together. Since the project had received extremely negative media attention upon the initial public announcement, we chose to keep the media and stakeholders apart for the duration of the project. Only the final celebration brought stakeholders and media back together.

The Power of Partnerships

One of the challenges of the project was befriending groups that were likely opposed to the project from the start. This requires the PR pro to "go behind enemy lines" and extend an olive branch first. If the PR pro takes the time to build relationships and sit in the opposition's monthly meetings (as I did with the area lake cleanup association), the walls begin to come down. We not only befriended the lake association, we grew the relationship to the point that ultimately the project team and lake association team worked together to clean up the lake every year. Each spring, the project brought volunteers, including engineers, geologists and other project leaders and their families, to the annual lake cleanup day. Area media covered the cleanup and together the two organizations - with different objectives - worked hand in hand for a mutual cause: lake cleanup. This spirit of cooperation generated numerous PR opportunities.

Social Media Amplification

The media would frequently grab photos and videos directly from our Twitter feed and use them on the local nightly news. The best part from a PR pro's standpoint: we created the content. (Our twitter feed, @BooneRepair, was deleted after the project's completion.)

One thing I discovered six years into the project was the power of "amplification." I would define "amplification" as key influencers and thought leaders (think powerful politicians and their social media teams) picking up our messaging and retweeting it. (In 2022, Twitter was the social channel of choice for many of the major politicians because it was so easy to use and to retweet.)

With timing and messaging planned well in advance, a message can gain strength and be amplified many times over. Social media becomes a well-choreographed "echo chamber." The constantly watched and measured data and analytics reflect positive numbers for all as a result of that amplification.

As we prepare for our final special VIP event and "swan song" before returning the area to the public for recreational use, we will plan the event amplification well in advance - retweet at this time, send kudos and congratulations at this point - so that well-planned back scratching can commence. To an untrained member of the public, one might just think the good politician is kindly heaping praise on a project. But to a professional communicator who has seen the power of politics up close, it is well-orchestrated choreography. The dance of a major infrastructure project and the stakeholders on whom its lifeblood depends commences and twirls and twirls....

SUMMARY:

- Stakeholders are great conduits for messaging.
- Build relationships: former adversaries can be colleagues.
- Social media is a tool – the photos and videos from it will be reused by the media.
- Use your social media feeds as an opportunity for the media to capture your high quality, safety-approved photos and videos of the project.
- Amplify your message through social media.
- Plan well in advance with influencers to re-tweet and share your key messages.

▶ 26 Fill the Dam Thing Up!

CHAPTER 7

The Media

The media must be kept up-to-date in numerous ways. We conducted biannual media updates: one in the spring and one in the fall. The media received the project e-newsletter and often directly turned the updates into news stories. Likewise, the media watched the project's Twitter feed and would use visuals, including photos and videos posted to Twitter, on the evening news. I managed the Twitter feed and it was also a direct source of news leads for the media.

Build a Viewing Platform

One very wily senior project leader had the foresight to direct crews to build a covered viewing platform that overlooked the work on the dam. The platform provided a safe location from which to shoot video and photos while keeping out of the way of the actual work. We "decorated" the platform with maps and graphics depicting project milestones. This made for a simple way to describe the project to new members of the media who were unfamiliar with the work, while showing construction in real time.

Reporter Churn

One challenge in today's media space is the constant churn of reporters. This can make things interesting in a multi-year project. Often, a new TV reporter would be covering a story that a veteran print reporter could practically write himself. So there was always a need to return to the basics at each media update with an explanation of the project from its start.

Maintain relationships with the local media. If possible, seek out a veteran reporter to help tell your story. I had this opportunity when a veteran returned to the local paper. Since he had reported on the story from its inception, I hinted to the editor that he would be a great choice to cover the project again. She assigned him to it and I thanked her profusely.

I recall one day when my boss urged all of us on the PR team to get on the phone and call our media contacts to pitch a story. In today's digital age, it's a nice touch to reach out from behind a screen and hear a friendly voice. The result of a simple conversation between an editor or producer and PR pro was excellent coverage from a talented project "veteran" as opposed to a new, cub reporter.

Boat Rides Do Wonders for the Soul

Our most memorable media event was the Saturday we offered boat rides to the media to showcase the work and improvements. We offered the rides in conjunction with the lake association's annual cleanup day. Our senior construction manager drove the boat and the project manager narrated the work during the ride. Our efforts to clear brush, mulch, and excess vegetation were very visible from the water.

It was actually one of our best media updates ever, as both project leaders and journalists relaxed on the boat tour. The media was, in a friendly way, held captive on the boat with us. So instead of short snippets and pivoting to their next story, we were able to take our time to explain elements of the project to them and they captured a different perspective of the project from the water. To this day, reporters from that ride remark on how much they enjoyed it.

SUMMARY:

- Create an e-newsletter and be sure all media contacts are on the list.
- If possible, provide a safe place to view and take photos/videos of the project.
- Maintain relationships with local media.
- Provide regular media updates.
- Create a fun event, such as a boat ride that provides a new perspective, for your media update.

30 Fill the Dam Thing Up!

CHAPTER 8

Everyone is an "Expert"

Hoover Dam Was Built in Two Years! What's Taking So Long?

When illustrating the importance of the seepage remediation project, our engineering team would cite the failure of the South Fork Dam in the disastrous Johnstown flood of May 31, 1889. The damage wreaked by an unbounded reservoir took approximately 2,200 lives.

One oft-repeated chorus of complaint as our project got underway was, "They built Hoover Dam in two years. Why should this project take so long?" What the vocal complainers did not consider was that 96 lives were lost in that project. Gambling with potential loss of life would be completely unthinkable today. In addition, infrastructure now falls under a slew of regulations with which the dam builders of yesteryear never had to contend.

Armchair Quarterbacks: The Importance of Frequently Asked Questions (FAQs)

Once you establish the public-facing email system, you will receive "fixes" from many "armchair quarterbacks." They may or may not have an engineering degree, but they will tell you how to fix your infrastructure issue! Just be prepared with polite acknowledgements. We received so many similar comments on our public-facing email system that we were able to group them together to create fairly standard answers.

If you receive enough questions, you can provide a "Frequently Asked Questions" or FAQs page on your website and newsletter. One way to disarm a potential adversary is to answer all his questions BUT be sure he does not feel he's receiving special treatment. When he asks 20 questions, provide him all the answers, but do so via the website so <u>all readers</u> are privy to what you say.

It Was That Dynamite!

Some people enjoy "conspiracy theories" or, at the very least, making up rumors. In the case of our neighbors, one such theory was that a road construction project several years earlier and at least six miles from the project, somehow "created" the dam's internal erosion issue. Our engineering team looked at this theory, studied it, and soundly dismissed it. But that did not stop the public! Early on, we were repeatedly bombarded by emails, comments, tweets, etc. telling us what they thought "created" the issue at the dam! We stuck with the facts in our key messaging.

SUMMARY:

- Be prepared for comparative questions ("What about XYZ project?") and have gentle answers.
- Listen for question themes and then answer them all together on the website so everyone benefits, not just a few loud complainers.
- People will say outlandish things. It's part of it!

CHAPTER 9

A Diverse, International Project, Chewing Tobacco, and "The American Way"

Our project was so large in scope that we would sit in a 40 x20 conference room around a 10 x 25 table in the main doublewide office trailer in a double ring of chairs - inner and outer. We used to joke that it was like getting to church in the South on Sundays… arrive early in order to get a seat in the back!

As a PR pro, I gravitated toward the outer circle (with apologies to Sheryl Sandberg, PR pros often prefer to observe those who "lean in"). I just like to watch the lead players in the inner circle. Typically, pre-pandemic, we would be packed in with 35 to a room. I remember conversing with colleagues who graduated from Louisiana State University or lived in Washington State. Others were from France, Italy, the United Kingdom, Morocco, and many other countries. Our common bond was a dam that had to be fixed. My job was to translate the highly technical language I heard - often in accented English - into terms our stakeholders and neighbors on the lake in Appalachia would understand.

International Project

A dear friend of mine was a civil engineer on the project. She loaned me books about drilling and grouting, as well as the original books on the dam's history. One day, I passed a man in the narrow hallway of the main office trailer. We greeted one another and a minute later, I heard the buzz of a text from my friend: "You know that book I loaned you on drilling and grouting? Well, that's the author!" she exclaimed. He was a renowned expert from the United Kingdom.

It was one more example of how the project was truly of international proportions.

Bear: It's What's for Dinner

Some readers may remember the old beef advertising slogan that went something like the words above. Working on a major construction site in Appalachia, I was exposed to foods and habits I had never seen during my days in corporate America.

Each year (prior to Covid), we held a chili cookoff where part-time chefs from all around the project came together, armed with crockpots, to show off their culinary skills. The "meat" of choice could be anything from traditional beef and chicken to venison and, yes, even bear meat. Sometimes the bear would be prepared and served separately at our luncheon feasts. The hunters got to share their stories and it all made for a fun time (unless, of course, you were the bear).

Chewing Tobacco

The vast majority of the Southerners who worked on the project chewed tobacco. That was a habit I had rarely seen before moving to construction. Now, as we sat around a conference room table, guys with old Styrofoam coffee cups in front of them would "let it fly," using the white foam container as a spittoon.

One of my beloved guards was an old Army guy who chewed tobacco. He had a great way of explaining things. One day he asked me, "Do you know why you learn to chew and not smoke in the Army?"
"No," I said.
"Because if you are on night guard duty and you light up a smoke, you get your head shot off," he explained.
I was wide-eyed.

Probably the most noticeable thing to me as an observer (other than just the sheer nastiness of the habit) was when a chewer needed his "fix," his leg would start to shake, much as a small child shakes when he urgently needs to go to the bathroom.

"I Did it the American Way"

I studied French in school and made a point to exchange pleasantries with the French project manager for the main contractor "en français." One day he was walking just ahead of me leaving our team's morning meeting.

"I did it the American way," he bemoaned to a colleague.
Uh, oh, I thought. What have we done?
And then he followed with, "I drove."
Sigh.

Normally, he walked everywhere around the site and he even had special walking paths created so he could walk safely to our daily morning meetings.

Unfortunately, Americans' love affair with our cars - to the detriment of walking and our waistlines - follows us in our reputation around the world.

From then on, I made a point, whenever possible, to walk with him and his colleagues to those morning meetings. My office trailer was close to their contractor trailer. There was safety walking in numbers as heavy equipment passed by and I, too, enjoyed the exercise and the short walk up the hill on the path he had specially made. Of course, we wore full PPE when walking anywhere on a construction site.

The Diverse "STEM" (Science, Technology, Engineering and Math) Camp

One of the best outreach events I recall from my time on the project was a STEM camp geared toward diverse high schoolers. Students who might not otherwise have been exposed to STEM and its associated careers had the opportunity to spend the month of June living in a college dormitory and learning from experts in the field from a variety of companies.

Each week, a different area employer offered a look into STEM careers, from health to manufacturing. Each company sponsored a week of activities for the participants. Students even learned to throw ancient spears on the college athletic field! One of the students' favorites was the day they were able to wade into a river with a team of fisheries biologists to gently "stun," hold, examine and measure a variety of fish. What a thrill to see young people, who likely never had the opportunity to examine "river critters" up close, find themselves falling in love with biology!

The students' experience culminated in a trip to Huntsville, Alabama to the space center. On the way, they stopped at an advanced manufacturing plant and heard an early recruiting pitch seeking them out as future workers.

SUMMARY:

- International projects combine cultures from across the world.
- Be open to differences in foods, habits, and culture.
- STEM is an international language.
- As a PR pro you can "speak" STEM by fostering youth interest. They may be your company's future workforce.

CHAPTER 10

Prepare for the Unexpected, From Break-ins to Blow-Ups

Firefighters

As I've mentioned before, I think public relations professionals are true adrenaline junkies. In my career, I've prepared for serious labor strikes and arrived for work shortly after someone threatened to blow the place up. If you want peace and quiet, best not choose our profession! I heard the great PR pro and crisis communicator Jim Lukaweski describe himself as a firefighter…always ready and prepared at a moment's notice, just waiting for the call! Here are just a few of the kinds of "fires" you may encounter on a major infrastructure project.

The Noise Man

The break-in occurred in a normal way. I kept my door unlocked so the public could have access to me. I had not thought through the fact that the "open door policy" made me "a sitting duck;" the spokesperson for a very controversial project had open access to her office.

I was in my office, working on my computer with my back to the door, when a man suddenly appeared screaming, ranting, and cursing. The two guards were on their front porch talking. They were out of earshot, outside and diagonally opposite from me, across the doublewide trailer from my office. I remember thinking, "This man could easily have a gun." I don't know how I managed it, other than by the grace of God, but I talked him out of my office and called a project colleague. I was so shaken. She said, "That's it. You lock your door from here on out." So, I did.

The entire "public access" portion of my job now meant that in order to see me, you went through the guards' entrance first. We placed a sign on my door to that effect. A few folks got mad: they didn't want to go through the guards to see me. But ultimately, as with any safety measure, people got used to it. And I felt safer. They also removed the solid door between the guards and me and replaced it with glass so at least they could see what was happening on my side of the trailer. We had a conference room - where we would host stakeholders and guests who stopped by - in the center room between us. The guards kept their coffee pot in there. Maps and project graphics lined the walls. It made a great space to host media and stakeholder updates and was now under the watchful eye of the guards.

"No Good Deed Goes Unpunished"

A few of the neighbors created an ongoing challenge for us early in the course of the project. In retrospect, one mistake we made was allowing one fairly technical neighbor an opportunity to visit the site and meet with our technical director. Rather than going away satisfied in the knowledge that we were working hard to solve the problem, he created a band of "three amigos" who stirred up as much dissension and noise as they could for several years. We met with them regularly and it wasn't until we gave them a "job" (assisting with neighbor outreach for our vegetation management program) that they finally quieted down. A long-time company representative had joined me for several meetings with this group and when I explained my exasperation, he gave me this outstanding piece of public relations advice: "No good deed goes unpunished, Mel," he said with a chuckle. I will never forget that!

"No People at Her Level"

The company representative was with me the day we gathered around a conference room table to meet the "three amigos." The meeting began with introductions and each of them going around the room and, in turn, telling who they used to be and the careers they had before they retired. Many well-to-do retirees from other states settled on the lake and they were only too glad to share that they "used to be" the CFO, CEO, etc. of companies up north and elsewhere.

The representative kept urging them to work through me, the assigned project communicator.

"We are not used to dealing with people at her level," they told him, as I sat there in silence.

Did I remind you that having "thick skin" is one of the most important traits of being a PR pro?

SUMMARY:

- Be prepared for the unexpected.
- Sometimes people are "set off" by a seemingly small thing. Have safety measures in place.
- When dealing with a negative person, try to find him a "job" volunteering in some capacity. It makes him feel included and his perspective can be helpful.
- Not every member of the public appreciates our role as project communicators. Have thick skin.

40 Fill the Dam Thing Up!

CHAPTER 11

Safety Rules: Pink Hardhats and Dressing for Success

The importance of safety on a construction site cannot be overstated or overestimated. Every meeting starts with a safety moment. Every job begins with a pre-job brief. We had 2-minute cards, "stop when unsure" procedure use, adherence postings, and post-job reviews. There was **"STAR"** (**Stop, Think, Act, Review**) and many other clever safety acronyms posted on badges and walls as a constant reminder of a safety-first culture. One of the best things I learned on the project was "stop when unsure." I use that safety phrase to this day, particularly when confronted with another car coming toward me in a parking lot. The manner of dressing is one more part of the safety culture.

Find Out the Company Uniform and Stick with It

When I first arrived at a construction site, I was very much a fish out of water. I wore riding boots and black dress jeans to a major special event only to receive a strong dressing-down (no pun intended) by a colleague who said, "Don't you know that we dress like the people we serve, Mel?" It was painful to hear. I was the person who always took pride in my beautiful suits while working as a marketing director at a major regional law firm. But construction is a completely different arena and you need only look around to get clues about how to dress.

One time I accidentally showed up in a suit when a vice president was visiting, thinking I would be "dressed up" for his visit. Whoops! The dress code for women in construction is jeans or khakis, long sleeved shirt (I typically wore the company's logoed shirt), and closed toed shoes – work boots if you are walking out on the site. Of course, Personal Protective Equipment including vest, ear protection, hardhat, safety gloves, and safety glasses is a must if you are walking around the project. Note for men: you will never have to worry about this! Not one time did I hear a man get a "dressing-down" for dressing incorrectly. This rule even applies for offsite visitors. Be sure you send them the safety dress codes in advance (closed toed shoes, long sleeves, pants). We once had a stakeholder show up on site with flip flops. Thankfully, she was able to retrieve a pair of tennis shoes from her car. The clothing lessons resonated and ultimately served me well. Lesson learned: always dress like the people you serve.

Pink Hardhats and Other PPE

In such a testosterone-rich environment, it's fun to show off your differences. In my case, I like pink. Some of the guys noticed that I like pink, as I often wore a pink logoed shirt. When a girlfriend saw a photo of me from when I first started the job – wearing oversized "man gloves" - she sent me fitted, pink safety gloves. I ordered pink composite-toed construction boots that were both comfortable and practical. And then, the ultimate surprise - a pink hard hat with "Mel" emblazoned across the front! The safety guys from the main contractor presented it to me and I was thrilled. I liked to joke that when I walked out on the job site it was like they belled the cat – when they saw the pink hard hat walking along, they knew they were likely being photographed for some public relations purpose!

SUMMARY:

- Safety should always be any project's top priority.
- Dress for "success" (safety) on a construction site.
- Maintain safety standards and protocol while showing your personality (in my case it was a pink hardhat, pink safety gloves, and pink work boots).

CHAPTER 12

Pro Tips: Scan Environment, Keep it Clean!

Scan Your Environment

A key term I learned in MBA school was "environmental scanning." It means keeping your eyes open to trends and patterns that can impact your project, from either outside or inside your company. In our case, as a result of environmental scanning, the issue of vegetation management rose to the forefront. From taking part in the community and neighborhood association meetings, we were able to foresee the issue. While the project team was busy working on designing and engineering a permanent fix for the dam seepage issue, a variety of vegetation was blooming all around the lake. As the lake came down, it exposed old trees along with fresh bushes and shrubbery. There was an irony to this that pitted one lake lover against another: fishermen who wanted a fish habitat vs. home dwellers who wanted a view.

Listen to, and Work with, Your Neighbors

We worked diligently with the two main lake organizations to reach out to the various neighbors. I clearly recall a day we were trying out some heavy equipment that would be used to mulch the brush along the shoreline. We were on public land near the project that had heavy vegetation. Our project manager and I were watching the equipment mulch a clearing on public property that left it looking tidy in no time. We had the president of the lake association with us and all agreed this was a good solution to offer to our neighbors. I was also planning an upcoming media event to showcase the equipment. The guys in charge of the equipment spoke to one another on two-way radios: one on the shore directing the man in the skid steer to start and stop. Later, this made for great media videos and photos as the equipment literally bulldozed and mulched the heavy growth!

No sooner had the lake association president left us than a man drove up in a pick-up truck, pulling a bass boat. He threw his truck into park a short way from where we were standing, jumped out, and yelled, "You're not going to do that on my property are you?!"
"Not if you don't want us to," calmly replied the project manager.
"I want my vegetation left for fishing," he said.

We assured him that would be fine and we would not touch his vegetation unless he wanted us to cut it. He left and headed off to the boat ramp.

This is one example of the importance of scanning the environment and "reading the room" in terms of neighborhood outreach. We did not cut or mulch in the fisherman's "yard," which included exposed shoreline and lake frontage.

We also embraced "the three amigos" (mentioned in Chapter 10) by meeting with them and seeking their ideas. They ended up being extremely helpful in neighborhood outreach during the mulching program.

All Hands Clean Up the Lake

Our outreach for vegetation removal was large scale. Two crews and a barge with a port-o-potty floated up and down the lake carrying a skid steer, a track hoe, and a man whose job it was to reach out to the neighbors through good old-fashioned knocking on doors and asking permission.

The boats helped us access hard-to-reach coves and we conducted regular, twice-monthly meetings with the neighbor groups and crews to determine any "hard spots." We would bring our boats and barges to the annual Saturday lake clean up where the guys, in an "all hands-on deck" effort, worked so hard to make the lake pristine.

SUMMARY:

- Environmental scanning will help you foresee potential issues.
- Listen carefully and pay attention to your neighbors.
- Get everyone together: workers, project leaders, and neighbors and "clean up!"

46 Fill the Dam Thing Up!

CHAPTER 13

Social Media and Public Outreach

Make it Easy for the Public to Access You

One of the easiest access points for the public is a simple email box. Let's say your project name is XYZ. You can create an info@xyzproject.com email address where the public can reach out to you directly with questions. You will be able to track the number of responses and kinds of questions you receive and it will also help with your environmental scanning process. What are the major issues? Do they clump together in some sort of bell curve? Can you address them directly in your next newsletter or tweet? The more you communicate with the public and assure them your project is moving along on time and on budget, the fewer concerned emails you will receive.

Create A Second Email Box if There is a Separate Topic

In our case, vegetation management was identified through environmental scans as a rising topic. A separate email box was created just for issues pertaining to vegetation management. That email went directly to the contractor who was hired to work as the interface between the boat crews and the public around the lake.

Social Media: Photos and Videos in the Public Space

Whenever you are using photos or videos in the public space, be sure you have the right approvals from your project leads before posting. Sometimes your safety manager will notice missing safety gloves on an employee or someone who is not wearing safety glasses. (After a while, you will become very good at noticing any missing personal safety equipment!) Once you have the correct approvals and post your photos or videos, they will "live on" permanently in the public space about your project. Hashtagging your project name (#ProjectXYZ) is a great way to search for photos and videos about it.

Newsletters are a great outreach tool

Generally, the media will use what is posted to the public feeds and newsletters directly and without asking permission, so be sure all photos and videos are approved and accurate. Initially we created newsletters weekly, then cut back to monthly and, eventually, quarterly as the project wound down. Newsletter programs allow for easy tracking of open rates and data analysis.

SUMMARY:

- Provide easy digital access to the project via its own public email.
- Make sure all project videos/photos are approved by your safety manager before posting.
- Hashtagging, #ProjectXYZ, allows for a quick project search
- Newsletter programs allow for easy tracking and analysis.

CHAPTER 14

Kindness and Ethics

Make Friends Wherever You Go

The idea of befriending people in the workforce seems like a simple one to me. If you are kind and use the basic principles your momma taught you – "say please and thank you" and follow the "Golden Rule" of "do unto others as you would have them do unto you" - you will be doing yourself a favor in the long run. I have found that the world can be a very small place indeed. Cultivate good relationships.

Hold Fast to Ethical Principles

During the project, we were not allowed to accept any gift worth more than $25. I recall once having a question and asking our project manager about it. A contact from a charitable organization wanted to give us a cooler, which was definitely worth more than $25. "If you have to ask the question," our PM said. "Then you already know the answer." Outstanding advice when it comes to ethics. Needless to say, I politely turned down the cooler.

The study and practice of ethics is ingrained in the Public Relations Society of America's accreditation process. I can still recite them: "Advocacy, Honesty, Expertise, Independence, Loyalty and Fairness."

In short, *Advocacy* is advocating and providing a voice for those we represent.

Honesty is telling the truth and advising your client to do likewise when communicating with the public. *Expertise* is honing our skillset through a continuous learning process. (The Public Relations Society of America offers an array of ongoing continuous education training opportunities.)

We maintain *Independence* by providing objective counsel to our clients.

A PR pro exercises *Loyalty* and faithfulness to her client while serving the public interest.

And finally, we use *Fairness* with clients, stakeholders, the media, and others as we respect the opinions of others and their right to free expression.

I followed these guidelines throughout the project.

SUMMARY:

- Make friends wherever you go.
- Follow the Golden Rule.
- Adhere to ethical principles in all you do.

CHAPTER 15:

Benchmarking and Focus Groups

Initial Research and Benchmarking

Just as the project's technical leads looked at projects from the Army Corps of Engineers at Center Hill and Wolf Creek Dams, so too did public relations look at the kinds of community relations and outreach conducted at other dam projects.

Conduct Stakeholder Focus Groups

Key to the success of the program is research. Customers and government officials are perceived as credible, trustworthy sources and their initial input is important.

Ongoing, open, two-way communications channels are essential.

Focus groups were conducted prior to my arrival on the project. Examples of some of the questions asked in focus groups:
- How do you want to engage with the project team?
- How do you want to receive information from project leadership?

The larger, overarching communications plan was developed after the stakeholder focus groups.

Tactical examples that came out of this and were carried forward throughout the project:

- Website
- Q and A on website
- Twitter feed*
- Monthly e-newsletter
- Onsite community relations office, open to the public
- The position of fulltime community relations person

*Twitter was chosen because of its immediacy and easy accessibility to the public. While Twitter allows for two-way communications and we always answered queries, at that time it tended to have fewer negative comments than Facebook. In fact, one time we saw this amazing tweet (see above) directed at a national network.

> **Brian Quesinberry@BrianQuiz**
> 5 days ago
> We have a TVA dam, Boone dam, and it is in need of repair due to seepage around the dam weakening it's structure. Lakefront home owners are upset that it is taking so long to repair and want them to hurry up. They don't care about the safety. Please do a national story on them!
>
> Hide conversation
>
> **NBC News** The costs of dealing with last year's near-disaster at the nation's tallest dam have reached $870 million, California's officials said. The total was pegged at $660 million in October.
> nbcnews.to/2rLe3AG

SUMMARY:

- Conduct communications research just as technical leads would.
- Benchmark against similar projects.
- Conduct focus groups with stakeholders. Your plan and tactics will emerge.

CHAPTER 16

The Very Rich: "He who has the gold rules."

"Let me tell you about the very rich. They are different from you and me. They possess and enjoy early, and it does something to them, makes them soft where we are hard, and cynical where we are trustful, in a way that, unless you were born rich, it is very difficult to understand. They think, deep in their hearts, that they are better than we are because we had to discover the compensations and refuges of life for ourselves. Even when they enter deep into our world or sink below us, they still think that they are better than we are. They are different."

"The Rich Boy"
F. Scott Fitzgerald

You may think it's odd to write a book on infrastructure with a quote about the very rich. When you work in public relations on a major infrastructure project, however - particularly one that involves a lake created by a dam - you will quickly find yourself surrounded by very wealthy people. As an example, a prominent NFL football team owner and businessman used to jet in for weekends on the lake. My husband, an avid pilot, used to tell me when he saw the famous football team logo on the plane's tail as it parked on the tarmac.

Rich people will be omnipresent in your life. They think nothing of picking up the phone to call the senator, governor, or CEO. You will do everything (within ethical means) to appease them and keep them from making those calls. I clearly recall cringing every time I saw the "West Palm Beach" area code pop up on my phone. That person was so threatening I had to advise the legal department.

Sometimes being neighborly meant rotating lights and building a sound barrier wall to protect them from the light and noise of the project. We learned to work together and cooperate with one another. We were going to be neighbors for a long time.

One of the neighbors told me many years before the project began, and it always stuck with me: "Do you know the golden rule, Mel? He who has the gold rules."

SUMMARY:

- Be prepared to deal with very rich or entitled people.
- These people are often your project neighbors. Listen to their concerns.
- Learn to work with them. When you are able, help them out.

CHAPTER 17

Transferrable Skills for Any Infrastructure Project

As infrastructure rises to the top of national conversation, I reflect on my community relations work for seven years with a major dam project. What I learned there is transferrable to any infrastructure project and the communities surrounding it.

Build Relationships - Get to know your stakeholders. Invite them to view and tour the project. Take time to meet with them on a regular basis. I regularly attended a monthly stakeholder group meeting throughout the project. It makes a huge difference to meet people and hear their concerns.

Be Responsive - Keep communication lines open. Listen and act. I can think of one neighbor I first met at a public meeting several years ago who now texts me on a regular basis. This neighbor has been an extra set of eyes and ears to call attention to matters my colleagues and I can easily address.

Build Trust - Warren Buffet famously said, "It takes 20 years to build a reputation and five minutes to ruin it." With trust comes a polishing of both your company's reputation and your personal brand. The Public Relations Society of America's Code of Ethics provides values to live by, not only for accredited public relations professionals, but for all who plan to lead community relations for infrastructure projects. Those values are:

Advocacy, Honesty, Expertise, Independence, Loyalty, and Fairness. Use these and you will gain and keep the trust of your community. (See Chapter 14.)

Lake Living - A Life of Privilege

My sole experience with "lake living" was as a small child. My family had a cottage on Conesus Lake in upstate New York. I remember with great fondness riding in the back seat of my father's Pontiac, sandwiched between my older brother and sister. Dad was driving, Mom was in the passenger seat, and we would sing "She'll Be Coming Round the Mountain" as we neared our destination, approximately an hour and a half from our home in Buffalo. I learned to swim on that lake and we spent many happy times at the cottage. To this day, we keep in touch with our dear, old neighbors. Upon reflection, those were good times and we were fortunate.

The lake dwellers I deal with on the project are completely different kinds of people. Let me share a few stories with you.

Building Rapport

I recall standing at the shoreline on a visit with a kindly, elderly neighbor. He showed me the docks and slides his grandchildren enjoyed during summers on the lake, prior to the drawdown. Then he said offhandedly while looking down at the lake, "I know who you built that sound wall for. Just so you know, the sound wasn't bothering us at all."

I can't recall the reason he initially asked to meet with me, but I remember his kindness always. Apparently, the feeling is mutual because even now he calls me with questions. I call him back to assure him and soothe his concerns. He frets as he watches lake levels change, even as they are supposed to in the good times.

It is amazing what you will find yourself doing as a community relations and PR pro for an infrastructure project!

"Love Thy Neighbor"
Troublemaker? Dissenter? Loud Mouth? Give Him a Job!

Every infrastructure project will have its share of naysayers; for us it was "the three amigos." One of our loudest naysayers from that group was a very bright person with a technical background. After numerous meetings and listening sessions with him, we realized all he wanted was two things:

- To be heard and
- To help in some way, i.e., "to have a job" (in a volunteer capacity, of course).

And that is exactly what we gave him: an opportunity for neighborhood outreach.

He and his team were able to go out in front of the cleanup teams and let the lake neighbors know when cleanup crews would be in their area. It was a relief to the PR and project teams to be able to provide peer-to-peer assistance with neighbor helping neighbor.

> **SUMMARY:**
> - Transferrable skills: build relationships and trust by being responsive.
> - People who live on lakes may feel privileged. Build rapport with them.
> - People just want to be heard. Listen and give the "noisy neighbor" a "job," such as lead volunteer. Their help and knowledge of the lake will be invaluable to you.

▶ 58 Fill the Dam Thing Up!

CHAPTER 18

Tearing Down, Starting Over

A Time to Tear Down

"There is a time for everything, and a season for every activity under the heavens…a time to tear down and a time to build…"
Ecclesiastes 3: 1,3

As I write this chapter, what remains of the project is being torn down. At the start of our weekly meeting, we were informed that all internet connections were going away. Only one conference room remained "wired."

The week before, we demolished a temporary Quonset hut that had stood onsite as a stalwart building and reminder of the project through the years. It was a gathering place for the workers to stay warm during their safety meetings on extremely cold mornings. It held tables and cubbies and tools. I knew its demolition would be of great interest to the media, so I posted a tweet one day ahead, on a Friday, that it would be demolished on Saturday morning. Within an hour, a member of the media contacted me to ask if he could come onsite to film the implosion. While that was not possible (shy of him getting a boat and camping out on the lake in front of the dam), I assured him I would be glad to provide video to him (and all members of the public) via our Twitter feed. His station aired the video and ran the story.

It was yet another outward sign of our continuing progress and the project winding down.

As I got out of my car one day toward the end of the project, I saw workers strapped in safety rigging. One of the workers explained they were preparing to remove one of the two main office trailers. The trailer that held the engineering teams for years would soon be gone.

Take Care of Your "Bodyguard"

There's an old expression that says "dance with the one who brought you" — in fact, Shania Twain wrote a song by the same name. The same goes for remembering all the kind folks who looked after you throughout the course of the project. It could be your custodian, your assistant or, in my case, an armed guard.

Yet another sign of the impending project conclusion was bidding goodbye to the guard who had been there for years. For a long time, we shared a trailer space, me in my office in one half, he and one other guard in their office space. They wore guns and were there to protect the project and, in theory, me, the person who faced the sometimes-angry public. Mainly, they served as good company for this extrovert as we worked in a trailer together on an isolated country road. Sometimes I brought them biscuits or coffee from McDonald's. I always made sure they got a free lunch when one was served up top for a safety or other work celebration. "You need to take care of your bodyguard," I would say, only half-jokingly.

And now it was time for him to go away as well. I took him and his helper a bag of his favorite apples, some mini cupcakes, and a thank you card.

"Where to next?" I asked. He did not know.

Repaving, Restoring

Sometimes, restoration can mean repaving and fixing the mess that you made. I put out a notice to all our boating and fishing contacts that the boat ramp adjacent to the project would be closed for a week for repaving, a much-needed restoration after years of heavy equipment moving through portions of it.

In one of the final months of the project, we met with the county roads superintendent for the second or third time. We met with him at the beginning of the project and assured him that although the heavy trucks driving back and forth would do some damage to his road, ultimately the project would make it right and provide repairs. There were handshakes all around and phone numbers and emails exchanged. Now was the time to make it right. Repaving made the roads new again.

"All We Can Do is the Best We Can Do Now" Charitable Giving: A Temporary Lifeline

The outpouring of support from our project to area charities was immense. Initially, we came together as an onsite team and committee. Our senior construction manager put himself on the committee, which, in turn, brought the top leaders from the contractors. The committee voted to support two local charities in a big way: the local food bank and the US Marine Corps Toys for Tots program. Each holiday season, special bins were available onsite to collect food and toys. Inevitably, they overflowed. We took an entire school bus, plus two pickup trucks full of toys, to the Marines. We helped the food bank by generating thousands of pounds of food.

Some of our project leaders would say, "What happens when we are gone?" to which our project foreman would reply, "All we can do is the best we can do now." Between our charity work and STEM outreach, we planted seeds for the future with a long-lasting impact.

> **SUMMARY:**
> - The end of the project will come. Tear down and move on.
> - Remember your "bodyguards" – the folks who helped you out - and bid them farewell.
> - Repave and restore – better than before.
> - Support local charities while you are on the project; you will have a lasting, positive impact.

▶ 62 Fill the Dam Thing Up!

CHAPTER 19

Tracking Progress: Spreadsheets and Plan B

Always Start with a Plan

Here is a sample from the strategic communications plan. I updated it annually and sent it to the project manager. I created shorter, task-oriented plans for smaller projects and events.

Goal:
Positive, proactive visibility and advocacy for both the dam project and the dam owner in the Tri-Cities region.

The company's community relations manager will provide ongoing community outreach using a variety of communications channels through the end of the project (no later than July 2022.)

Strategy:
The overarching communications strategy for the dam was to build transparent communications with the community and stakeholders in order to build confidence and trust in both the project and in the parent company. This is mainly accomplished through one-on-one relationship building with key stakeholders.

Create a Simple Spreadsheet to Track Your Progress

One of the handiest tools I used on the project was a simple Excel spreadsheet that I updated prior to the weekly, and later biweekly, managers meetings. The spreadsheet enabled me to track ongoing projects along with due dates and who was responsible for that action. I color coded it with what was coming up and what was complete. This simple tool was a great way to keep the project manager updated on all the community relations activities for the project.

Public Meetings: Don't Scream into the Mic!

I came on board two months after a very public meeting that was well publicized in all local media. The headline of the local newspaper, *The Johnson City Press*, read: *"Boone fix: 5-7 years, up to $300 million. The Tennessee Valley Authority unveils massive plan to repair Boone Dam."* (Note: cost was later adjusted, final project came in on time and under budget.) That meeting solidified the need for an on-site community relations person.

One lesson learned from the initial public meeting: "No open mics!" When members of the public get an open mic, it provides an opportunity to grandstand in front of a large audience.

Although they may yearn for that opportunity later (I had lake neighbors at subsequent meetings ask me where the mic was), the ideal setup for future public gatherings was small areas of discussion with every aspect of the project represented. We were able to use that effectively to help engage the neighbors while quelling potential for grandstanding.

We met in public high schools with easy access and parking for the community. We set up tables around the cafeteria with input from different areas of the project (construction, engineering, natural resources, dam safety, etc.). We invited our partners, like the state wildlife organization, the local fishing clubs, and neighborhood associations to provide displays as well. In addition, we provided computers and index cards for comments and we invited people to sign up for the project newsletters.

Always Have a "Plan B"

Be Flexible: No Running Water? You are on a Construction Site!

As I write this and the project is winding down, I had a meeting at the job site. I was happily drinking coffee all morning on the drive to the site from my handy "to go" mug. When I arrived, I was greeted by our construction manager who said, "Hello, there is no running water." That suddenly brought new meaning to "to go!"

From time to time on construction sites, water lines are cut. For me, there is a personal threshold: always have a "Plan B to Pee." Thankfully, there was an office just down the road that had running water, so I headed there to work until it was time for the project meeting. Office workers who disdained port-o-potties found their way to a convenience store around the corner when water was "on hold" (and their bladders were not!)

SUMMARY:

- Start with a plan.
- Keep track of all your community relations with a simple spreadsheet.
- Place subject matter experts around the room in a public meeting so people can interact with them. This prevents grandstanding.
- Flexibility is key on a construction site.

66 Fill the Dam Thing Up!

CHAPTER 20

The Power of Dreams

Stress, Pressure and Dreams of the Wrong Way

Toward the end of the project, I dreamed I was making a hard-right turn onto an exit ramp. The only problem was all the cars were coming at me, off the ramp. I was driving directly into traffic. I didn't need a dream analyst to figure this one out! It was time to leave. The stress and pressure of years on the same project had built up and were taking their toll. I found myself up in the middle of the night, sipping organic tea and wondering just how I was going to "get it all done." We were in the middle of planning a major celebration, a "grand finale" event. It had been my dream to have a giant celebration for the public when the project ended. I used to call it "Bluegrass and Barbecue" as I visualized hundreds of folks eating barbecue and listening to live Bluegrass music on the lawn in the public beach area of the lake.

We were stretched so thin on manpower that I didn't know how we would actually accomplish such a yeoman's task. I was relieved when shortly after my fitful dream, word came down from the highest levels that we would host a VIP/stakeholder event for only about 150 people and then open the site to the public that afternoon with the help of project leads and project partners.

We began rethinking the final event plan on a much smaller scale.

And mentally, I turned my car around and made for the exit.

Cockroaches, Cornell, and the End Game

I was a competitive swimmer during my college days at Cornell. I lived in what best could be described as a "tenement" on Stewart Avenue in Ithaca, New York during my sophomore and junior years. I lived with five other girls and two or three (depending on the week) of their boyfriends on the third floor of a building that urban legend said was originally a house for priests. I lived in the "shower room," a tiny room with a slanted roof, a dormer, and tile walls.

When I returned to campus early after Christmas break to practice, I was all alone in that large house. Except for the cockroaches, that is. Coming in from the pool, I flipped on the lights of our dark kitchen and the roaches scurried up the walls. I vividly remember lying on the couch one day after practice and putting my gum on a piece of paper on the coffee table next to me so I could take a nap. I turned my head, opened my eyes, and stared straight at a cockroach enjoying my well-chewed Juicy Fruit.

I later joined a sorority and was able to live in Ithaca's "Collegetown" my senior year. It was an apartment near the bagel shop with three of my Kappa Kappa Gamma sisters and an occasional boyfriend. I may as well have moved to Park Avenue, the difference in living conditions was so striking!

Why do I tell you this? Because my mother commented years later, "Honey, I knew how much you wanted to go to Cornell because I saw where you were willing to live when you first moved there."

Sometimes in life we must put up with something uncomfortable in the short term as we keep the end game in mind.

Feeling Disheartened and Sticking it Out: Remember, it's the Long Game that Counts

As I write this, I am speeding toward the finish line of what can no doubt be considered a marathon. I am on the last few miles now and in an all-out sprint. We will play host to a VIP and stakeholder celebration event commemorating the project's success and its safe return to the public. I once read that the "middle miles" of a marathon race are the toughest. If you are a full-time communicator on a major infrastructure project, stick it out. Who knows? In the end, you may end up writing a book about your experiences and be able to share your helpful insights with others!

> **SUMMARY:**
> - Short term discomfort can lead to long term gain.
> - At times you will feel like quitting. Stick it out for the long haul.
> - YOU may be writing the next book on your fabulous infrastructure project!

70 Fill the Dam Thing Up!

EPILOGUE

Have a Vision

When I first began to plan the final special event to commemorate the reopening of the public swimming and recreation area at the dam, it was Fall 2021. I posted a screen saver photo to my computer that I looked at every time I logged on: it was the beach and swimming area as it looked in July of 2014. The more I looked at it, the more it became my goal. This was the "finish line" we were all headed toward.

The Power of Team

In his seminal business book *Good to Great*, author Jim Collins says the key to success in business is "putting the right people on the bus." Four dynamic women created the core committee for the final event commemorating the completion of this major infrastructure project. We enlisted the help of people from across the company, as well as outside partners, to create a memorable finale.

Part 1: Executives and Stakeholders

The late May day was sunny and warm. We had about 150 guests, including stakeholders and company representatives, present to share in the joy of a completed project. The C-suite executives delivered their remarks flawlessly, without looking at their prepared notes. The media scrum gathered around the company leaders to grab interviews with the repaired dam as backdrop. Everyone enjoyed a boxed lunch under a giant tent. We also provided opportunities to interact with project leads and partners at separate booths in a pavilion and under pop up tents.

Once the VIPs left, we had two hours to "turn the site around" and welcome the public.

Part 2: Welcome Back to Boone Dam: The Public

At 3 pm, when I looked up and saw the stream of cars begin to filter down the long driveway, my eyes grew teary. This — the reopening of the dam for the public's enjoyment — is what we spent nearly seven years working so hard to attain. We had subject matter experts from across the company, along with external partners, standing by to greet people and answer questions. Displays included huge fish tanks loaded with lake fish, small robots used to inspect the dam, and computer models of the repair— a veritable "show and tell" of the entire project. Technical leads and local wildlife representatives stood alongside neighbors, who — no longer adversarial —enjoyed telling people how we worked together to produce a great result. It was a final opportunity to share with the public the story of our amazing seven-year project that finished both on time and under budget.

I eagerly waved a greeting as I saw my husband's white pickup truck round the corner. He and our 19-year-old son were there to tour the booths, meet our subject matter experts, and neighbors, and see the lake and dam from the viewpoint only workers had shared these past seven years.

As I stood there waiting for my family to park and start their walk around, I recall feeling like a party host to the small parade of people walking past me en route to the booths.

"Welcome back," I greeted people with a smile as they filed past.

One family with several children timidly approached me and asked if they could go swimming in the lake.

"Of course!" I exclaimed. Youngsters immediately began jumping and skipping into the lake until soon there was a crowd of people frolicking in the water.

Boone Dam was back.

▶ **74** Fill the Dam Thing Up!

SPECIAL COVID INSERT:

COVID-19: Thoughts on Working Through a Global Pandemic

People often recall milestones in time; key points in their life history. Covid-19 was one such moment. I took note of the feelings I wrestled with working through a once-in-a-century global pandemic. Upon reflection, it was a time of resilience building. What follows is one person's experience of working through that time.

Pandemic Pivot

The first part of the year 2020 was much like any other. In January, I was fortunate to receive a service award from a local university and had an opportunity to celebrate with friends and family. In February, our family visited Washington, D.C. to see my mother and sister. That turned out to be the final time I saw my mother. We had a wonderful visit and even toured the Library of Congress. My sister, a Washingtonian through and through, always insists on some sort of educational "field trip" while we are there and even though my mother had reached the age of 99, we simply seated her in a wheelchair and took her along with us! As I write, I am drinking coffee from the Jefferson Memorial mug, rimmed with cherry blossoms, that I purchased in that wonderful gift shop.

Fill the Dam Thing Up!

As March rolled around, news of the virus that was spreading around the world was taking shape in the U.S. My colleague, an engineer on the project, and I were scheduled to take part in a large "STEM-posium" event for high school girls to be held at the local university. She was the keynote speaker and we had multiple booths planned for the girls to visit and participate in hands-on activities and learning.

But the rumblings of a killer virus were drawing closer. We did not know whether we should even take part in the event.

We conferred the night before with our project manager, who said we should decide based on our own feelings of safety and risk. It was March 12, 2020.

We moved forward, and although several of the girls' schools decided to cancel, there was still a good crowd and my colleague went on with her keynote speech. The girls loved her story of coming to this country from Venezuela at age 10, not speaking any English and seeing math as the "common, universal language." As we were preparing for her speech, however, I heard rumblings from university friends that the school's president was calling his direct reports together and potentially shutting down the university.

We had lunch in the crowded college cafeteria. I recall wondering if I would be able to continue doing this much longer (as it turned out, I did not eat in a large crowd for more than a year).

For some reason, I couldn't get internet service in the newly refurbished student center, so I walked outside. It was then that I saw the note from one of our company vice presidents: no meetings or gatherings in groups of 10 or more.

It has been my experience that when a vice president tells you what to do, you better do it! I returned inside and told the STEM-posium organizer that I thought we needed to cut it short. I knew some of the women had to travel a couple hours to get home and this would give them extra time to stock up on groceries or necessities (I guess we all treated this like an impending snow storm!). We cut the event short and sent people home.

I recall walking in the house and my son, then a junior in high school, saying, "They are shutting down the NBA." The shock of that news resonated with me. The NBA? When did professional basketball ever shut down for anything?

We all, as Americans, learned to pivot. I was directed to take "work from home" training early the following week. I watched a mandatory training video and got the sign-off from my boss to begin work from home.

Every week when I had an office in the trailer, I would write out and plan the next week on my white board. I remember looking up at that white board and wondering how long that same date would be frozen in time? I packed up what I thought I needed and took a few digital photos of items I would refer to, like project codes for billing.

And then on March 17, 2020, I headed home. As I write this, I have been working from home for two years. With the exception of occasional onsite meetings, the majority of my work and interaction with coworkers is now on computer screens and Webex, Teams, or Zoom calls.

The shock of suddenly being thrown from a routine was startling. I found myself passing by the refrigerator and near the kitchen often and I quickly put on seven pounds. (Glad to say I was able to shed those seven pounds and return to my "1995 marrying weight" just over a year later!)

The good news for me was that my son was around. While a sudden thrust into "virtual school" was an enormous shock for him, we had one another to navigate this new world. As the pandemic wormed its way into his senior year in high school, I remember saying to him, "Who would have ever thought your senior year would be your homeschool year?"

We were always close and we enjoyed our times "meeting up" in the kitchen over lunch or snacks. There was plenty to talk about in both the world and the United States, so we had the chance to talk and reflect together in what amounted to "social studies (and life) lessons with Mom." My husband kept working in a traditional office and we looked forward to his arrival each evening.

The Global Pandemic, The Olympics, and The Loneliness

As I write this, we are in the middle of the 2022 Winter Olympics. Last night, 21-year-old U.S. champion figure skater Vincent Zhou posted a video to Instagram announcing he would not be allowed to compete in the men's individual programs due to a positive Covid test. My heart ached for this young man whom the Olympic skating commentators said "got up at 4 am every day for years to pursue his Olympic dream." As he spoke from isolation, he said he had stayed away from everyone and had no idea how he could have gotten the virus. He talked about his loneliness and the sadness poured from his heart.

There was something about his candor and authenticity that resonated with me.

As someone working on a major infrastructure project during a global pandemic, I watched it transition from work on a bustling site with more than 200 people onsite (and many others working offsite) to moving to on-camera meetings, wrapping up the largest portions of the project and staying miles apart. Our work became tiny windows on a screen and our faces (or often only our voices and names) were all that could be seen of the human touch. I say that about voices only because people, particularly in the technical fields, tend to turn their cameras off during meetings. The PR team members - generally "people people" - like to make eye contact and for the most part keep their cameras on. Of course, there are exceptions and good reasons to keep cameras off. Sometimes we are eating during a noon meeting or have small or sick children close by.

Work from Home Challenges: Keeping in Touch

Particularly at the start of the pandemic, young children were wandering in and out of the camera as they adjusted to "homeschool" and parents working at home. Just recently, I found out a coworker had a baby a few months ago...how did I miss that? As life moved onscreen, the traditional touch points of "the before times," like bumping into office coworkers in the hallway, went away. Today's "water cooler conversation" is the two to three minutes of personal sharing you can squeeze in with coworkers before the Webex meeting convenes. Just yesterday, except for seeing my husband in the morning, I interacted with no one in-person all day. I waved to neighbors at a distance when I walked my dog. My husband worked until 8 pm, so for a 12-hour stretch, it was my dog and me and people appearing in dots on tiny windows of my computer screen. No wonder people went so crazy adopting pets when the pandemic hit! There are times I do not know what I would do without my dog - he's not only a great companion, but he also keeps me walking and moving, no matter the weather!

Everybody's Somebody's Somebody

I heard that line once. It's never been truer but less visible than during a pandemic. As we enter our third year of working from home, I realize how many life events I have missed because I wasn't bumping into someone in the normal course of daily work interactions.

Just yesterday, a colleague mentioned he would be gone two weeks from work. When I asked why, he said his wife was getting ready to have a baby.

Catching Covid

Since I went home from my onsite trailer office on St. Patrick's Day 2020, I conscientiously did everything in my power to avoid getting Covid. I added zinc and vitamins D and C to our daily regimen. For one year before the vaccine was available, I adopted the life of a recluse. People used the word "bubble" to describe the trusted friends allowed to share their personal space. For me, it was a bubble of four: my husband, son, and my son's girlfriend. Even when a dear friend wanted to come into my home to share the joyful news that her grown son and his wife were expecting a baby, I invited her to sit across the room and both of us wore masks. When her husband came in to install our dishwasher, I opened all the windows. I never let a workman in the house without all of us being masked. When my neighbors invited us to dinner, we politely declined. Instead, we began a routine of leaving food for one another on our front porches. My friends knew my level of fanaticism.

Once the vaccine became available, we breathed a collective sigh of relief. We (mistakenly, as it turns out) thought everyone would run to embrace the shot that would get us out of the morass. But we were wrong. A simple shot and face covering became politicized and weaponized and the state where the infrastructure project is located had a very low rate of vaccination.

As I write this chapter in February 2022, I am recovering from Covid. I am fully vaccinated and I received the booster shot. I truly have no idea how I caught this! My level of vigilance in attempting to avoid the virus is second only to someone who hid in their house the entire time. I did go out but always masked when indoors.

On Tuesday evening, I felt a bit of a scratch in my throat but I pushed myself to run three miles. (I generally run twice a week.) It was cool and breezy that evening and when I got home and took a hot shower, I recall sitting in the living room, freezing cold and so tired I was unable to move. Our gas log fireplace was not working at the time and I wanted so badly to just sit by the fire. The following day, I had a slight cough and did not think much of it. I went for a walk with a friend and my dog in a local park. I mentioned to my friend that I had a slight cough and deliberately did not embrace her. The following morning, I woke up with what felt like a full-blown cold. I told my husband I would go get a Covid test to be sure I didn't have it, as I had an in-person meeting with a large group of people the following day.

I contacted a friend who is a nurse to determine what to do. I had never needed a Covid test. She directed me to the "drive through" walk-in clinic that included a telehealth follow up visit with a physician.

On Thursday, I had my first "up the nose" experience with a Covid test. A long swab is inserted up each nostril by a fully PPE-outfitted nurse. "I've got this cold," I told her. "Just want to get it checked out to be sure." She probably heard that many times a day. I had barely driven away, donned my N-95 mask, and headed into the grocery store to buy cough drops, when the doctor rang in on my phone. The service was sketchy in the store and he asked me to call when I got home and could see him on camera. The telehealth call back puts you in a queue and he rang in as I got back home, unloading fruit and cough drops.

"Well, you have Covid," he began, while looking at the computer screen in front of him. "What?" I said. "I am boosted, vaccinated, and I feel like I have a cold!" True disbelief. Two solid years of avoiding and evading the coronavirus that had taken over the world and now it was inside of me.

The doctor assured me that the PCR test they used is extremely accurate. He also said the virus was "endemic" and all of us would deal with it annually from here on out. Much like colds and the flu, Coronavirus had settled in to stay.

After hanging up from the telehealth, I called my husband. Then I called the friend I had walked in the park with.

Then I asked a buddy at work what the protocol was. I sent a message to my new boss, who was in an important board meeting. "What is the topic and nature of your request?" she wrote.
"My health," I put simply. She stepped out of the board meeting and called me.

I entered the company "protocol" and she supplied me with a form to fill out. Suddenly, I would become one of the reported numbers that day. As I stared at *The New York Times* coverage map for my county that I received every day, I knew I was one of the positive cases for the first time. I looked at the full map of my home state that looked like a sea of dark purple…the darker colors indicating more Covid cases.

My boss was very kind, got someone else to fill in for my media duty, and I began to rest. I was back working from home the following Monday.

▶ 82 Fill the Dam Thing Up!

AUTHOR'S NOTE:

Trusted Counselor: Here then Gone

Several years ago, while self-employed, I ran all the communications for a woman who would become a prominent judge in the region. I saw her photo in the paper one Saturday morning while sipping coffee. (I still subscribe to a paper copy of the newspaper and read it in addition to the digital version when I can.) In the photo, she was standing on a spiral staircase in her black robe with two other robed judicial colleagues. It was an announcement that she and the others planned to run again. I snapped a photo and texted it to her with my congratulations along with the question "Where have 8 years gone?"

A few hours later, she texted back, wishing me, my husband, and son - whom she called by name - all the best. I had not seen her in eight years, as is the nature of my work. Here, then gone. A PR pro is trusted counselor and confidante to political clients and, on a project, its leaders. All their secrets can be shared and kept. As President Harry Truman once said, "The buck stops here."

There is a decisive end to a political campaign - Election Day.

In the case of a seven-year project – it is complete and once again, turned back to its former state.

And then, as in politics, the PR pro moves on.

▶ 84 Fill the Dam Thing Up!

Acknowledgements

I would like to thank my beloved, late parents Jesse and Marie Plubell who always encouraged me to write. To my beta readers: Mark Brown, APR, who saw the very first manuscript and still managed to say some nice things about it; Rick Boggs, an old Cornell friend and engineer, and Rebecca Henderson, a published author and avid reader. Thanks to my editor, Rebecca Horvath, and my friend Nancy Williams, both published authors who helped me navigate the maze of publishing. And thanks to my business coach, Sue Painter for always pushing me forward. Thank you to the many friends I made along the journey of a seven-year construction project. I learned so much from each of you. And finally, thank you to my husband, Dan, who lovingly described the project as, "my dam job," and who kindly let me disappear into my home office to write early each morning.

86 Fill the Dam Thing Up!

About the Author

Mary Ellen Miller, APR, is a results-driven public relations and marketing strategist with over 30 years of experience. She has led award-winning community relations programs, developed strategic communications plans, and managed crisis communications for a variety of clients, including large enterprises, universities, and government agencies.

One of Miller's most notable accomplishments was leading the community relations program for a seven-year, $400 million dam infrastructure project in Northeast Tennessee. Miller worked closely with local residents and project leaders to ensure that the project was completed on time and under budget. The project was a success, and it continues to have a positive impact on the economic development of Northeast Tennessee.

Miller is a graduate of Cornell University and East Tennessee State University. She is Accredited in Public Relations (APR) by the Public Relations Society of America (PRSA). She is also a founding member of the PRSA's Tri-Cities Chapter.

Miller lives in Johnson City, Tennessee with her husband and her dog, a Jack Russell mix. They have one son in college.

You can find Miller at marketingmel.com and on social media.

Made in United States
North Haven, CT
27 August 2023